BUG BOOKS

Pillbug

Stephanie St. Pierre

Heinemann Library
Chicago, IL

Customer Service 888-454-2279
Visit our website at www.heinemannlibrary.com

Design: Kimberly R. Miracle and Cavedweller Studio
Illustration: David Westerfield

Originated by Dot Gradations Ltd
Printed and bound in China by South China Printing Company

12 11 10 09 08
10 9 8 7 6 5 4 3 2 1

New edition ISBNs: 978 1 4329 1236 9 (hardcover)
                     978 1 4329 1247 5 (paperback)

The Library of Congress has cataloged the first edition as follows:
St. Pierre, Stephanie
 Pillbug / Stephanie St. Pierre
     p. cm. -- (Bug books)
 Summary: Describes the physical characteristics, habits, and natural environment of the pillbug.
 Includes bibliographical references (p.   ).
  ISBN 978-1-4329-1236-9 (hardcover) -- ISBN 978-1-4329-1247-5 (pbk.)
  1. Armadillidium vulgare--Juvenile literature. [1. pillbugs.] I. Title:
 II. Title. III. Series.
  QL444.M34 S72 2001
  595.3'72--dc21
                          00-12400

Acknowledgments
The publishers would like to thank the following for permission to reproduce photographs:
© Animals Animals (Donald Specker) pp. **4, 7**; © Bruce Coleman pp. **6** (Robert Dunne), **10** (Dwight Kuhn); © Corbis pp. **17, 18, 19**; © Dwight Kuhn pp. **8, 15, 21, 26, 27, 29**; © James P. Rowan pp. **20, 23**; © James Rowan pp. **14, 22**; © NHPA pp. **11, 12**; © Oxford Scientific Films (Robert Jackman) p. **28**; © Peter Arnold Inc. (Clyde H. Smith) p. **5**; © Photolibrary (Barrie Watts) p. **9**; © Photo Researchers Inc. pp. **13** (Biophoto Associates), **16** (G. Buttner/Naturbild/ Okapia), **24** (Holt Studios International), **25** (Ken Brate).

Cover photograph of a pill Pillbug reproduced with permission of Photolibrary.com (Marshall Black).

The publishers would like to thank James Rowan and Lawrence Bee for their assistance in the preparation of the first edition of this book.

Every effort has been made to contact copyright holders of any material reproduced in this book. Any omissions will be rectified in subsequent printings if notice is given to the publisher.

Contents

Some words are shown in bold, **like this**. You can find out what they mean by looking in the glossary.

What Are Pillbugs?

shell

leg

Pillbugs are small, grey bugs. They are not **insects**. They are **crustaceans**. They have seven pairs of legs and a rounded shell.

4

A pillbug's shell is called an **exoskeleton**. The exoskeleton (shell) protects the soft parts of the pillbug's body.

What Do Pillbugs Look Like?

Pillbugs have two short **antennae**. When they are rolled into a ball they are about the size of a pea. They have seven pairs of legs and a rounded shell.

It's hard to see a pillbug's belly. When they are bothered, pillbugs roll up into little balls. Pillbugs are sometimes called roly-polys. They are called pillbugs because they look like pills.

How Are Pillbugs Born?

Female pillbugs lay eggs. Most pillbugs have two **broods** of young each year. They have one brood in the spring and another in the summer.

egg

Pillbug eggs **hatch** in a **pouch** in their mother's belly. There can be 200 eggs in the pouch. They hatch after three to seven weeks.

baby pillbug

egg

How Do Pillbugs Grow?

The **female** pillbug carries her babies in a **pouch** for over a month. The babies are white and their bodies are soft. They only have six pairs of legs.

old skin

new skin

As the pillbugs grow, their shells get too tight. The old shell falls off and there is a new one underneath. This is called **molting**.

adult

baby

When pillbugs **molt** for the first time they grow another pair of legs. Now they have seven pairs, like an adult. Pillbugs molt a few times before they are fully grown.

Baby pillbugs are very pale. Their shells get harder and darker each time they molt.

shell

How Do Pillbugs Move?

Pillbugs crawl. They move very slowly. They cannot run away from danger. Pillbugs can roll up instead of running away.

pillbug

Pillbugs are **nocturnal**. This means
they usually only move around at night.
During the day they often sleep under
rocks and logs.

What Do Pillbugs Eat?

This pile of grass clippings makes a perfect meal for pillbugs. Pillbugs also eat dead leaves and old fruit. They even eat rotting logs.

16

Sometimes pillbugs eat growing plants. Pillbugs can damage plants if they eat their roots and new leaves.

roots

17

Which Animals Eat Pillbugs?

shrew

Pillbugs have many enemies. **Shrews**, toads, frogs, and lizards eat pillbugs. Small owls and some foxes also eat them.

Spiders, centipedes, and some beetles also eat pillbugs. Pillbugs even eat other pillbugs that are **molting**.

centipede

Where Do Pillbugs Live?

Most **crustaceans** live in water. Pillbugs live on land but they need to stay **moist**. If they get too dry they will die.

Pillbugs do not do much when it is cold. They hide under rocks and logs and stay still until the weather warms up.

Why Are Pillbugs Special?

Pillbugs roll up when they are disturbed. You can pick one up gently and see how it rolls.

You can keep pillbugs as pets. Keep them in a jar with holes in the lid. Put some **damp** soil in the jar. Feed your pillbugs leaves and potato peelings. Spray the jar with water every week.

Thinking About Pillbugs

Which of these animals is related to the pillbug? Can you think of any other animals that have an **exoskeleton** (shell)?

28

This boy wants to keep some pillbugs as pets. Where should he look for them? What should he feed them?

29

Bug Map

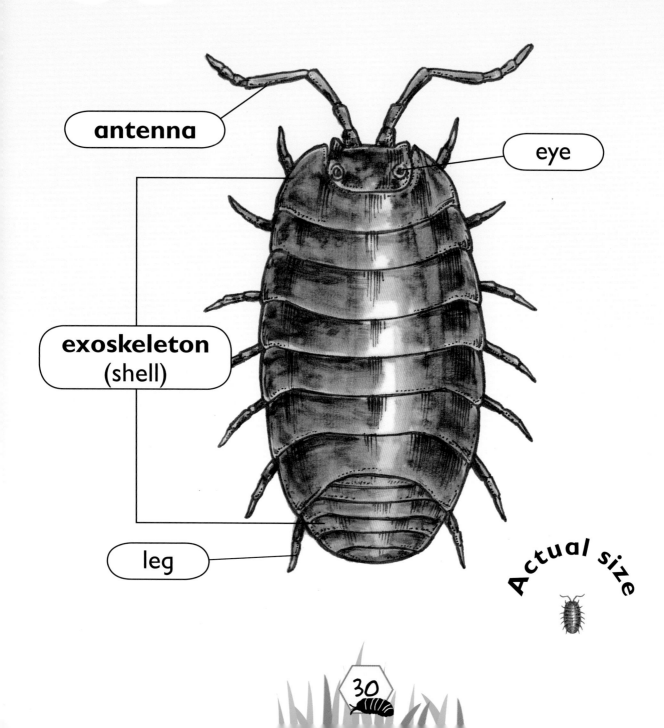

antenna

eye

exoskeleton
(shell)

leg

Actual size

Glossary

antenna (more than one = antennae) thin tube that sticks out from the head of an insect. Antennae can be used to smell, feel, hear, or sense direction.

brood group of babies that hatch at the same time

crustacean relative of insects that has a tough shell. Pillbugs, shrimp, lobsters, and crabs are all crustaceans.

damp a little bit wet

exoskeleton hard shell on the outside of an animal's body

female animal that can lay eggs or give birth to young. Women are females.

hatch break out of an egg

insect small animal with six legs and a body with three parts

moist slightly wet

molting time in an insect's life when it gets too big for its skin. The old skin drops off and a new one is underneath.

nocturnal being active at night, and sleeping during the day

pouch baggy area of skin where a mother carries her young

recycle take waste and make it into something useful

shrew animal that is related to a mole. It eats insects and other bugs.

Index

More books to read

Harris, Nicholas. *First Library of Knowledge: World of Bugs.* Farmington Hills, MI: Blackbirch Press, 2006.

Ross, Stewart and Jim Pipe. *Going on a Bug Hunt.* London: Franklin Watts, 2006.